DEAD BUT
LIVING

Understanding Christ's Life in You

DEAD BUT LIVING

Understanding Christ's Life in You

RAY SAMMONS

GALATIANS AND JAMES REPHRASED

FORWARD BY DR. BILL MOUNCE

Dead But Living™
Copyright © 2015 by Ray Sammons

This title is also availalbe as an ebook product.
Visit www.deadbutliving.com/ebooks

Requests for information should be addressed to:
HAWKEYE.PRO™, LLC
1007 N. Sepulveda Blvd., Manhattan Beach, CA 90267

Sammons, Ray
    Dead But Living : Understanding Christ's Life in You /
Ray Sammons.
        p. cm.
        ISBN-13: 978-0-9965621-0-2 (softcover)
        1. Devotional literature, English

Printed in the Unisted States of America
15 16 17 18 19 20 21 22 · 14 13 12 11 10 9 8 7 6 5 4 3 2 1

Contents

Forward

Every once in a while a new type of book comes along that helps us understand and apply God's Word. This is such a book.

Many people have translated the Bible, written paraphrases to help you understand its meaning, and compiled reference books to supply background and commentary. In as much as I am involved in all three endeavors, I would certainly affirm the importance of each. However, *Dead But Living* is in a different category, combining elements of all three.

While it is not a Bible, it is based on the Bible and conveys the author's understanding of God's Word.

It is somewhat like a paraphrase, but it goes beyond even what most paraphrases do. Sentences are rearranged. Explanations added. Insights included.

While it is not a reference book, it does include many interesting background facts and pictures that will help the message come alive in ways that perhaps you have not experienced.

The end goal of *Dead But Living* is to help us all understand and rejoice in the fact that, in the words of Dietrich Bonhoeffer, the gospel bids us come and die; and yet it is only those who die in Christ who truly live. We live with Christ, and in community with one another.

May this book truly help you see this.

Dr. Bill Mounce
President
BiblicalTraining.org

Dr. William D Mounce (Ph.D., Aberdeen University) lives as a writer in Washougal, Washington. He is the President of BiblicalTraining.org, a non-profit organization offering world-class educational resources for discipleship in the local church. See www.BillMounce.com for more information. Formerly he was a preaching pastor, and prior to that a professor of New Testament and director of the Greek Program at Gordon-Conwell Theological Seminary. He is the author of the bestselling Greek textbook, Basics of Biblical Greek, and many other resources. He was the New Testament chair of the English Standard Version translation of the Bible, and is serving on the NIV translation committee. See www.BillMounce.com for more information.

Introduction

Dead But Living is a book about the most important issue of life: how to be accepted by and at peace with God. To explain how this is possible, two books of the Bible, Galatians and James, have been re-phrased for the twenty-first-century reader.

Part 1 of the book is Galatians re-phrased. This letter details how to be spiritually dead yet still be alive from God's perspective. The first rule God gave Adam and Eve was to not eat from the Tree of Knowledge of Good and Evil, and punishment for violating that rule carried the death sentence.

Part 2 is the letter from James to the Jews around the world, re-phrased for Gentile readers. This letter gives some instructions about how to live our lives once we are dead but living.

You will find this book mentally stimulating at the very least and life-changing at best.

Part 1
Galatians Rephrased

Why we are dead, from God's perspective, and how
we can regain life.

DATE: AD 57

FROM: Paul of Tarsus, Corinth, Greece

TO: Christians in Galatia

RE: The false teachers in Galatia

Paul is in Corinth writing to the Galations

Please share this letter with each of the churches in Galatia.

Galatia was in the middle of modern Turkey

I am surprised to hear you have allowed some Jewish teachers from Jerusalem to come to Galatia and teach that all believers in Jesus must be circumcised. I am even more surprised that some of you are transferring your allegiance to this perversion of the gospel. Therefore, I am writing this letter to again share with you the good news about Jesus.

I understand those false teachers are saying my teaching is wrong because I have never had any instruction about the gospel. So I'll begin by reviewing the source of my knowledge.

Paul's Education

I did not get the gospel I preach from the leaders of the Jerusalem church. The gospel I preach came directly from Jesus. Let me explain.

> I did not get the Gospel that I preach from the leaders of the Jerusalem Church.

You know the kind of person I was fifteen to twenty years ago. I hated the people who were perverting the laws and traditions of our fathers by following Jesus. When Jesus was traveling around preaching, I was in Jerusalem studying to become a Pharisee under the great teacher of the Law, Gamaliel. After Jesus was crucified I tried to destroy his followers and his teaching. I was more zealous than anyone my age and I directed the Sanhedrin-Guard to drag men, women, and whole families to Jerusalem before the Sanhedrin for punishment.

Paul's Conversion[1]

I was on my way to Damascus, accompanied by some of the Sanhedrin-Guard, with orders from the Chief Priest to find the followers of "the way," bind them with chains, and take them back to Jerusalem

---

1   Some of the details about Paul's conversion from the book of Acts have been added to the narrative to help the reader understand Paul's claim that he did not get his Gospel from the church leaders.

Galatians [15]

Jesus himself appeard to me for punishment. As we approached Damascus, Jesus himself appeared to me and said he had chosen me to proclaim his gospel to the Gentiles. That was the hardest moment of my entire life: I discovered first that Jesus was alive, and second that he wanted me to go tell Gentile sinners they could be his followers.

I was so shocked that I did not return home. Instead I went into the Arabian Desert and stayed there for three years. It was there that Jesus revealed himself to me little by little. He revealed the gospel to me and I learned about his plan to forgive both Jews and Gentiles equally. I also learned he had revealed his plan long ago in the Scriptures and I had missed it.

When my training was finished, I went back to Damascus and started teaching what I had learned. The Jews there would not accept me or my teaching. It got so bad that they were waiting at the city gates to kill me, so some of Jesus' followers lowered me down a back wall of the city in a basket and I escaped.

> **They lowered me down a back wall of the city in a basket and I escaped.**

Then I went to Jerusalem to see Peter; I stayed with him for fifteen days, and I met James also. The Jews learned I was in Jerusalem and they started trouble, so I left and began preaching the gospel in Syria and Cilicia.

The Jerusalem Council

About fourteen years later, after Barnabas and I had finished our first missionary trip, the trip where we met you, God revealed to me that I should go to Jerusalem and share with the church there the gospel I was preaching. Barnabas and Titus went along on that trip.

> **They did not require our friend Titus, a Gentile, to be circumcised.**

At first we met with the church leaders in small groups, explaining to them our gospel and what God was doing for the people we were teaching. Peter, James, and John, the pillars of the church, did not add anything to my gospel. They understood what God was doing through us and they did not require our friend Titus, a Gentile, to be circumcised. I should add, however, that some spies from the

The Jerusalem Council

The trip to Jerusalem Paul describes, the one where Barnabas and Titus went along, is called the Jerusalem Council. This happened in AD 49–50, and it is also recorded in Acts 15. This is arguably the most important council in the New Testament because it confirmed that Gentiles don't need to become Jews to be accepted into the church. In fact, the church today is predominately Gentile.

Most of the members of the church in Antioch—Paul and Barnabas' home church—were Gentiles, and some Jews from Jerusalem arrived insisting that Gentile Christians must be circumcised to be accepted by God.

Paul and Barnabas were adamant that the Gentiles didn't need to be circumcised or follow the Jewish laws to be accepted by God. To solve the disagreement, the church sent Paul and Barnabas to Jerusalem to consult with the leaders there for an answer.

There, Paul and Barnabas met with Peter and James (and probably others), explaining that the uncircumcised Gentiles were accepted by God. The whole church was called into session and three major things happened:

First, Peter explained that God sent him to preach to some Gentiles and God gave them the Holy Spirit just the same as he did to the Jews (Acts 10).

Second, Paul and Barnabas explained how God accepted the uncircumcised on their missionary journey.

Third, James, Jesus' brother, spoke, saying the conversion of the Gentiles was exactly what the Old Testament prophets had predicted. God was calling out a people for himself from the Gentiles!

James' confirmation that Peter and Paul's experiences were prophesied in the Old Testament concluded the discussion. The consensus was that the church should not make it difficult for Gentiles to become Christians.

Sanhedrin infiltrated our meetings and tried to get us involved with circumcision. We did not listen to them even for a moment.

When we left, Peter, James, and John shook hands with me and Barnabas, telling us to continue preaching to the Gentiles and that they would continue preaching to the Jews. The only thing they asked was for us to help the poor, especially the poor in Jerusalem, and we were already eagerly doing that.

Paul Corrects Peter

Instead of being taught by the leaders of the church, I had to correct them. When Peter came to visit us in Antioch, he ate his meals with the Gentile Christians just like we did. But as soon as some followers of James came from Jerusalem, Peter went back to the Jewish tradition of refusing to eat with Gentiles, even the Christian Gentiles. Barnabas also started following their example. When I found out about this, I stood up in the next public meeting and corrected Peter, saying,

> *Why do you now ... practically force these Gentiles to live like Jews?*

"Peter, you were born a Jew, but you have been living like a Gentile. Why do you now urge and practically force these Gentiles to live like Jews? You and I are both born Jews, and not mere Gentile sinners, and we ourselves have learned that we can't have a right standing before God by keeping our own Jewish laws.

"Both you and I have been teaching that observance of the Law is not essential to being right with God. Now if we, by word or practice, suggest that keeping the Law is essential, we nullify the gospel."

The Gospel

"As we both know, nobody can keep the whole Law, therefore the Law condemns us to death; it demands that we die to pay for the laws we have broken. The good news is that Christ obediently died in our place, and therefore, through our reliance on him, we died to the Law. Since we are dead before the Law the Law has no control over us, the Law is useless to us. We are now free from the Law to live for God."

Since we are dead before the Law the Law has no control over us, the Law is useless to us.

Let me make a personal example. When Christ was crucified, I (and every believer) was crucified through him before the Law. So now as I live, the Law sees me dead with Christ; now I live in complete trust in and reliance on the Son of God, who loved me so much that he died in my place.

Therefore, we must not treat God's gift as something of minor importance. We should do absolutely nothing that would set aside, invalidate, or frustrate our gift from God.

I am very concerned about you folks in Galatia; I'm concerned about your lack of good judgment. When I was there you understood the meaning of Jesus' death as plain as if I had waved a placard in front of your eyes. You not only understood it but you relied upon it and were filled with the Holy Spirit.

The Holy Spirit

Now let me ask you a question about those days:

"Did God give you the Holy Spirit because you were keeping the Jewish Law? "

Did God give you the Holy Spirit because you were keeping the Jewish Law?

Of course not!

You received the Holy Spirit after you understood Jesus' death and you trusted him to save you from the penalties of the Law.

Let me ask another question: If trying to obey the Jewish laws could not give you eternal life in the first place, why do you think trying to keep them now will make you stronger Christians?

Consider Abraham

Consider the experience of our father Abraham, the first Jew. He lived before the Law was given. He had the same experience we have had. God made him fit for heaven because he believed what God told him.

God gave Abraham a promise and he wrote it down. Part of his promise looked forward to the time he would save the Gentiles by their faith when it said, "I will bless those in every nation who believe me as you do."

> God gave Abraham a promise and he wrote it down.

Therefore, in God's eyes all of us who rely on Christ are partners in fellowship with Abraham.

Consider the Law

Please take a close look at what the Law says. When God gave the Law, 430 years after his promise to Abraham, it came with a curse on those who rely on keeping the Law to gain a right standing before God. It says, "Cursed is everyone who at any time breaks just one of the laws written in the book of the Law!"

Cursed means they are devoted to destruction and doomed to eternal punishment.

The Great Exchange

Christianity is the only religion in the world where the believer is declared acceptable to God without "doing anything." In Christianity, becoming right with God is a free gift. It's given to everyone who accepts the death of Christ in exchange for their own death.

THE BAD NEWS

God gave his laws to Moses, and these laws describe the highest quality of life humans can live here on earth. Any failure to live the high-quality life is called sin. Further, the Law says that anyone failing to live the high-quality life deserves to die. The culminating bad news is that no one can live the high-quality life; everyone has sinned and, therefore, everyone deserves to die.

THE GOOD NEWS

God made us, he loves us, and he knows we cannot live a life without sin. Therefore God sent his Son, Jesus, to earth to demonstrate how to live without sin. The Law could not condemn him to death because he did not sin. God declared he would accept Jesus' sinless death in exchange for all the sins in the world—past, present, and future. God made peace between himself and the world by Jesus' death, and he no longer holds people guilty because of their sins! That's good news!

THE GREAT EXCHANGE

"For God took the sinless Christ and poured into him our sins. Then, in exchange, he poured God's goodness into us!" (2 Cor. 5:21 TLB).

The Good News

The good news is that Christ has bought us out from under that impossible Law by becoming a curse in our place. The Scripture says anyone who hangs on a tree (is crucified) is cursed.

> *The Good News is that Christ has bought us out from under that impossible Law by becoming a curse in our place.*

Answer me this: Why would anyone in their right mind and with good judgment try to gain a right standing before God by keeping the Law when they know the only way to have a right standing before God is by believing him?

The prophet Habakkuk, who lived 1,400 years after Abraham understood this, said, "The man who is declared right before God because of his faith in God's promise shall live."

God gives men a right standing before him when they rely on Christ, therefore he can give this right standing to Gentiles as well as to Jews. Now all of us, both Jews and Gentiles, can have the Holy Spirit through our reliance on Christ.

God's Contract

I know some of you are having a problem with this because the same God who made the promise to Abraham also gave the Law to Moses. Let me illustrate the connection with an example. When a man signs a written contract, he cannot later change his mind, break the contract, and decide to do something different. God operates the same way.

The Law which came 430 years later cannot void the contract.

God made a contract with Abraham and his child. Note the contract was not with his children, meaning all Jews, but with his child. He made the contract with Abraham and Christ. This means that the Law, which came 430 years later, cannot void the contract and make a new and different way to have a right standing before God.

Why the Law Was Given

The logical question then is this: If God's contract with Abraham is still good, why did he give the Law to Moses? The answer is simple. He gave the Law to show us Jews just how guilty we are before him. It was our teacher and our guardian, until Christ came.

Now that Christ has come, we don't need those laws to guide us to him.

Now in Christ Jesus we are all (both Jew and Gentile) sons of God because of our faith in Jesus. In Christ there is no distinction between Jew and Gentile, slave or free, male or female; we are all Christians, and we are all one in Christ.

> *It was our teacher and our guardian, until Christ came.*

Now that we belong to Christ, we are his children. Since we are Christ's children, we are descendants of Abraham, and all God's promises to Abraham apply to us.

A Will

Here is another way to look at our Jewish relationship with the Law. In normal life, when a father dies and leaves a large, valuable estate to his underage son, the son is not much better off than a slave. He is under the protection of guardians and must do what they say until he grows up. That is the way it was with us. Before Christ came we were like slaves, following the guidance of the Law.

The Gospel

At exactly the right time, God sent his Son, born to a human mother, under the Law, so that he could buy our freedom from the Law and adopt us as full-grown adult sons. Consider what this means.

> *At exactly the right time God sent his son..., so that he could buy our freedom from the Law and adopt us as full-grown adult sons.*

We are not slaves to the Law any longer; now we are God's own adult sons! And since we are his sons, everything he has belongs to us. All of us are heirs of God because that is the way he decided it should be.

You Gentiles have the same kind of history; before you knew God, you were slaves to so-called gods. You followed special rules and observed certain days, months, and seasons according to the traditions of gods that really did not exist. Now that you have found God, or I should say now that God has found you, you are free from these gods. You, too, are sons of the true living God. You, too, are heirs of God.

Don't Change the Gospel

I am staggered by the thought that you want to add to Christ's death by being circumcised and that you Gentiles want to revert back to pagan practices. When I hear these things about you, I wonder if the time I spent with you was wasted.

> I am staggered by the thought that you want to add to Christ's death by being circumcised.

I'm sure you remember that I was sick when I first preached the gospel to you. In fact, that was the reason we stayed so long in Galatia. I vividly recall that you did not reject me then, even when I was sick. You accepted me as an angel from heaven, or Jesus Christ himself! You would even have plucked out one of your eyes and given it to me, if it would have helped. What has happened to that good relationship we had then? Have I become your enemy because I tell you the truth?

Ishmael and Isaac

Those of you who want to be under the Law, do you really know what the Scripture says? Consider this illustration: Abraham, our spiritual father, had two sons, Ishmael and Isaac. There was nothing unusual

about Ishmael's birth. His mother was Hagar, a slave, and he was born in the ordinary course of nature.

Isaac's birth is another story. His mother was a free woman, Abraham's wife. At just the right time, when she was ninety years old, God gave Sarah the son he had promised her twenty-four years before.

The point of this illustration is this: we who come to God ... are free from the Law and we are acceptable to God.

In this illustration Ishmael's mother, the slave, is like present-day Jerusalem, the mother city of the Jews. She represents all the people who are trying to please God by keeping the commandments. All those people are in bondage; they are slaves to a system of rituals.

Isaac was born to Sarah, the free woman, and she represents the heavenly Jerusalem, the mother city of those who come to God by faith. You and I are like Isaac; we are born into God's family because of the promise God made to Abraham.

Ishmael was fourteen years older than Isaac, and he despised and persecuted his little brother. It is the same today. Those of us who are born of the Holy Spirit are persecuted by those who want us to keep the Jewish laws. But remember what the Scripture says happened to Hagar and Ishmael. Sarah said, "Get rid of that slave woman and her son, for that slave woman's son will never share in the inheritance with my son Isaac" (Gen. 21:10 NIV).

The point of this illustration is this: We who come to God because of our faith are not cast out like Ishmael. No, we are like Isaac, free from the Law and acceptable to God because of our trust in and reliance on his promise.

Not under Law

We Jews are free from the Law and you Gentiles are free from the bondage of imitation gods because Christ has paid our debt and set us free. If you allow yourselves to be circumcised or if you try to earn God's favor by ceremonies, you offend Christ.

In fact, if you start relying on circumcision to earn your position before God, you must keep every other part of the Law without one tiny slip. You

can't earn God's favor by having some faith and keeping some of the Law (the part you select). With God it is all one way or the other. You must keep all of the Law without one slip, or you must rely completely on God's promise through faith without any effort to keep any part of the Law.

> *If you rely on circumcision or any other ceremony to make you right before God, then Christ's death cannot save you.*

Let me say that plainly: If you rely on circumcision or any other ceremony to make you right before God, then Christ's death cannot save you from God's eternal punishment!

Because this is so serious, I beg you to not listen to those false teachers who have come to you. They have not come with God's message.

Apply the Gospel
Now some conclusions:

• Christ set us free, and this gift of freedom brings a new set of responsibilities.

- Since we are trusting God to save us (both in this world and in the next), we have the responsibility to be responsive to and controlled by the Holy Spirit so we can experience all the good things God has planned for us.

> *The Holy Spirit will guide us to help each other and thereby fulfill the Law of Christ.*

- To help us, the Holy Spirit implants in each of us a set of new character traits:

      Love, joy, peace, patience, kindness, goodness, faithfulness, gentleness and self-control.

- As we let the Holy Spirit guide us, we will experience the satisfaction of these traits in our lives every day.

- The Holy Spirit will guide us to help each other and thereby fulfill the law of Christ.

- If by chance a Christian among you gets entangled in some misconduct or sin, a group of you who are responsive to and controlled by

the Holy Spirit should gently and humbly restore and reinstate him. Do this without any show of superiority, and be on guard so that one of you does not fall into the same temptation.

• If anyone thinks he is too busy or too important to shoulder somebody's load, that person is important only in his own eyes. He is deceived and cheats himself.

• Each of us has his own load of little oppressive faults. Therefore we must do our very best, and when we have done the best we can, we will have the personal satisfaction of a work well done. We will have done the things that are worth doing and we won't need to compare our work with anyone else's work.

• When someone teaches you the Word of God, you should help him by paying him for his time.

• The man who tries to deceive God only deceives himself. God will give each person a harvest of exactly what he sows. If he sows to satisfy his own personal desires, apart from God, then he will reap decay and ultimate destruction.

- If a man is relying on Christ, he will sow to satisfy the Holy Spirit and he will reap all the benefits of everlasting life. Therefore, whenever the opportunity presents itself, do good things for anyone (something profitable, something that is for their spiritual advantage), and especially for our Christian brothers.

Salutation

I've taken the pen from the scribe and I'll finish this letter in my own handwriting.

Notice how large I have to make the letters.

Those teachers who want you to be circumcised do it to avoid the persecution that comes from relying on Christ. They want to boast about your submission to them.

God forbid that I should boast about anything or anyone except the Lord Jesus Christ. Since I was crucified with him, my interest in the attractive things of this world was killed long ago, and the

world's interest in me is also long dead. Because of his cross it does not matter if we are circumcised or uncircumcised. What matters is that inside is a new and different person.

Slave Scars

I want God's mercy and peace to be your everyday experience. From now on please follow my instructions about these matters. Remember that I carry the scars of the whippings from Jesus' enemies that mark me as his slave.

The grace of our Lord Jesus Christ be with your spirit.

Sincerely,

Paul

Galatians Background

Paul was in his late fifties when he wrote this letter to the Galatians, which was his first letter, and he was in his late sixties when he wrote 2 Timothy, his last letter.

A few years before this letter was written, Paul and Barnabas had visited Galatia on their first missionary journey and established new churches there.

When this letter was written, Paul was on his second missionary journey (with Silas and Timothy) and he was living in Corinth, the sin city of his world. He also wrote his letter to Rome while he was in Corinth.

In Corinth, Paul was receiving word that some Jews from Jerusalem were traveling to these new churches and telling them they must be circumcised to be acceptable to God. He writes this letter to refute that error.

Unlike his other letters, Galatians has no references to specific people. The consensus was the church should not make it difficult for Gentiles to become Christians!

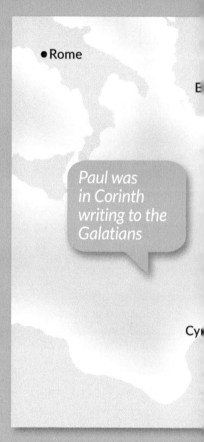

• Rome

E

Paul was in Corinth writing to the Galatians

Cy

Part 2
James Rephrased

How to live the high-quality life since we are dead but living.

DATE: AD 45-49
FROM: James
TO: Gentile Christians around the world

Greetings.

Would you like your spiritual life to be
perfect, complete, and not wanting
anything? Then rethink your reaction to
your occasional difficult events. Instead of
complaining about them, greet them with joy,
because these events give you steadfastness. So
stay with it. Stay on course. (1:1-4)

*Rethink
your
difficulties*

If rejoicing about difficulties seems like a mystery,
then ask God for wisdom on how to put it into
practice—he'll give you some ideas to follow and
he won't be upset that you asked. When the ideas
come, act on them. They are God's answers to your
prayer.

If you waffle and don't act on his answers, it means
you really didn't expect an answer in the first place,
and therefore you'll continue to be uncertain about
God's leading in all the other phases of your spiritual

life. If you act on God's answers, then you'll have the internal happiness that comes from the conviction that God is for you and is helping you experience his happiness. God rewards steadfastness with the best life possible. (1:5-8, 12; vv. 9-11 are included in other sections)

Ask for wisdom

When you are tempted to do evil, that temptation comes from your lack of steadfastness, from your mistaken idea that doing something evil will make you happier than doing something good. But evil temptations do not come from God. God is perfect. Evil cannot add anything to his experience of happiness, therefore God is not tempted by evil and he does not tempt you to do evil.

The good and perfect opportunities come from God, and he does not change. Here's the proof: God decided (of his own free will) to give us the Bible so we can be born again, and once we are born again we become his prize possessions. Why would he tempt us to do evil? (1:13-18)

————

Don't show any anger

To continue your steadfast living, be eager to listen to others' problems, don't be in a hurry to give advice [but give it when it's needed], and by all means don't show any anger—your anger will never produce the righteousness of God. Steadfast people don't live wickedly; rather, they live by God's Word, knowing it will save them from the inner turmoil wicked people experience. (1:19–21)

————

Read, study, and meditate on God's Word, and then do what it means to you. That is the way to remain steadfast. When you are doing what you know to do, you will be happy doing it. If you are not happy helping orphans and widows [or whatever else his Word speaks to your heart] or doing God's Word, it will show up in the snide and filthy things you say, and with that attitude all your efforts will not produce the inner happiness and joy you desire. (1:22–27)

———

Living, as we do, by faith in our Lord Jesus Christ—the Lord of glory—it's wrong to rank people in your meetings according to their net worth, and it's wrong to arrange the seating in your meetings according to rich or poor. If you do so you've become a judge honoring some and dishonoring others. God has chosen the poor to be rich in faith and heirs of the kingdom the same as he has the rich people. There is no difference. When you distinguish between rich and poor in your meetings, you dishonor what God has honored. These very rich whom you've honored are often the ones who drag you into court and speak evil of the God who has called you. (2:1–13)

———

Demonstrate your faith by what you do

We demonstrate our faith in God by the things we do. We are like Abraham. God considered him righteous because he believed him (had faith), and he demonstrated that faith by the things he did (leaving home as God indicated, having a son as God promised, offering his son as God directed, and on and on). We also demonstrate our faith [or lack of it] by the things we do.

Rahab, the Old Testament prostitute, demonstrated her faith when she hid God's messengers from their enemies.

If the things we do don't demonstrate our faith in God, then our friends and others will consider our faith worthless and our lives meaningless. (2:14–26)

Before you become a teacher, remember that teachers are always held to a higher standard than their students.

Teachers should set the standard by watching what they say! No one should bless the Lord on Sunday and then curse people during the week. Blessings and cursings from the same mouth is not acceptable behavior! (3:1–12)

Bless, don't curse

If you want the benefits of real wisdom, then keep God in charge of your life. Live well, help people around you, speak well of people, and don't brag about what you do or flaunt your good deeds.

It's your "walk" and not your "talk" that builds a reputation for wisdom.

God's wisdom for how we relate to other people is pure wisdom, not contaminated with deception or half-truths. It will produce the greatest happiness and completeness known on this earth in the people who understand and apply it.

Keep God in charge of your life

Nothing can be better than God's wisdom (it is pure), therefore it can be relied upon to produce "perfection" in your lives. Acting out God's pure wisdom will make you the most complete, happy, self-actualized, contented people on earth. You will need nothing else. Your heart and soul could not be more satisfied, and you will learn from experience that there is nothing better than God's wisdom!

Using God's wisdom you'll have an attitude of wanting to get along instead of quarreling, and you'll be gentle with other people's feelings. You won't use harsh or demeaning words, and you'll be open to reason. You'll listen to other people's ideas even when they give you admonitions or corrections.

Use God's Wisdom

Using God's wisdom you'll extend mercy to needy people. You'll help people you know need help or who ask for it.

Using God's wisdom you'll seek out places to help—visiting prisoners and hospitals, repairing fences, loading moving boxes, lending money, giving rides, and loaning your "things." You'll actively seek ways to help because you are happiest when you are helping.

God's wisdom will allow you to be impartial in your dealings with friends and neighbors. You will not need to "take sides." You will be able to hear disputes without becoming emotionally involved. Therefore your advice and reactions will be sincere. (3:13–18)

By keeping God in charge of your life (and being steadfast), you will avoid the quarrels and disappointments other people have. God's love for you is so strong that he will provide you wonderful, loving directions to steer you through your everyday life. You won't become entangled in activities and associations that diminish your enamorment with him. (4:1–10)

Friends, if you condemn other Christians for the way they follow God's leading, you are condemning the directions God has given. It's best for you to follow the leading you have and not judge others for the leading they have! (4:11–12)

Don't plan your life as if God does not exist

Hey, don't plan your life as if God does not exist! It is good for you to travel and earn your living, but it's not good to do that without involving God and then brag about your achievements. From now on acknowledge God, ask for his direction, and then go earn your living. Remember, when you know what good thing you should do and you don't do it, you are committing a sin! (4:13–17)

Now I have a few things to say to some rich people, not because you are rich, but because of the way you obtained your riches and what you are doing with your gain. You live as if there is no God, you cheat your employees, you hoard what you have, you ignore the needy, and you live in luxury

thinking only of yourselves. You have no intention of changing your behavior, so my advice is to get ready for God's judgment that's coming upon you—cry and groan about your future. Before God the riches you have hoarded and the way you obtained them will be used as evidence against you. That's their only value! (5:1–6)

———

To my friends who make an honest living I say keep it up until the Lord returns. You are like the farmers who plant their crops and then wait for the spring and summer rains. You are like the prophets who delivered the Lord's message and then suffered through any repercussions. Remember, don't grumble about each other in this process or you will be judged by the Lord for whom you wait. Also remember that we honor those who endure the most in this lifetime. Consider Job and how the Lord's mercy and kindness helped him.

Say "Yes" or "No"

As you steadfastly live out your life, be true to your word. Don't try to add to your character by swearing or taking an oath. Be the kind of person who says "Yes" or "No" and then lives up to their

word. Don't say, "By God this" or "By God that" or
"By (anything)." If you swear or take an oath it will be
counted against you on judgment day. (5:7–12)

———

If you have put God in charge of your
life, then share your feelings with him.
If you are in trouble, tell him so in your
prayers. If you are happy, then tell him
so by singing (in your heart or at the
top of your lungs).

Share your feelings with God

If you are sick, then let God minister to you through
the elders of the church. Call for them to rub oil
on you, under the Lord's authority, and then pray
for you. If God has finished building your character
through your sickness, then you will get well. But
in any case any sin in your life will be forgiven.
(5:13–15)

———

If you feel someone has done you some wrong, then
go to them, share your feelings, and pray for each
other so God can mend your relationship.

If God is in charge of your life and you understand what he wants, then ask him to use you to accomplish his objectives. The Old Testament prophet Elijah understood what God wanted and his prayer caused a three-and-a-half-year drought. Later he prayed again and the drought was over. (5:16–18)

Share your feelings pray for each other

—————

If you see someone wandering away from God, do what you can to rekindle their appreciation of God. Reuniting people with God will save them from destruction and their sins will be forgiven. (5:19–20)

Signed,

James, a servant of God and of the Lord Jesus Christ

James Background

The book of James is a letter written to the first-century Jews who were living all around the Mediterranean Sea. James was Jesus' half brother and a leader in the Jerusalem church, along with Peter and John. Some of the dispersed Jews came to the Passover in Jerusalem every year and James listened to their problems and concerns.

James sent a letter to these dispersed Jews before any other New Testament book was written.

James's letter is not one continuous story; rather, it reads like the dictionary or the book of Proverbs. It changes the subject often and without introduction.

James writes to Jews knowing his readers will fill in the gaps in his thoughts and understand what he is saying. For example, he refers to the Old Testament characters of Abraham, Rahab, Elijah, and Job, sure his readers know their stories.

Readers must decide when James is using a hyperbole or a metaphor, and when he's to be taken literally. For example, he says the tongue is a fire, life is a mist, and gold will rust. James also uses fifty-three words not used anywhere else in the Bible.

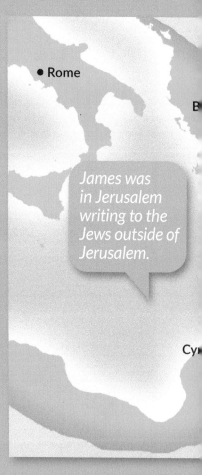

• Rome

B

Cy

James was in Jerusalem writing to the Jews outside of Jerusalem.

About The Author

Ray Sammons lives in Tucson, Arizona, with his wife, Phyllis. In 2015 they celebrate fifty-seven happy years together.

Dr. Sammons holds a Bachelor of Theology degree from Multnomah University, Portland, Oregon, and an MS and PhD in Agricultural Economics from Montana State University, Bozeman, Montana. He has been a Jesus follower since 1940 and combines his theological and economic training into practical Christian living. His book Job—The Finest Man in All the Earth treats Job as a rancher and businessman on cosmic display, demonstrating why and how men worship God for who he is and not for what he does.

He is now retired after teaching at three universities, traveling twice around the world on consulting projects, and operating his own business for twenty years.

Dr. Sammons is an elder in the Presbyterian Church, has served as interim pastor, and has taught Sunday school classes for many years.

He is a student of the apostle Paul's life, and in 2007 he toured Turkey and Greece following Paul's footsteps. The photographs in this book are from that 2007 trip.

Study Resources

In this information age we have ample resources to learn more about living the high-quality life. Millions of people live at peace with God, and many of them offer help to others for how to do it.

Below is a short and by no means exhaustive list of places to get free ideas, inspiration, and training about living the high-quality life.

- **BiblicalTraining** (www.biblicaltraining.org)—Their goal is to help make fully formed followers of Christ. This site has the highest quality information available online. It's free, there is enough material for a masters degree, and it is all taught by experienced, qualified staff.
- **BibleGateway** (www.biblegateway.com)— BibleGateway is a free online site to read, research, and reference Scripture on your desktop, laptop, tablet, smartphone—anywhere—in more than 770 languages and more than 50 English Bible versions!
- **Blue Letter Bible** (www.blueletterbible.org)—Blue Letter Bible provides powerful tools for an in-depth study of God's Word through their free online reference library (21 Bible versions, 23 commentaries, and 10 Bible dictionaries), with study tools that are grounded in the historical, conservative Christian faith.
- **e-Sword** (www.e-sword.net)—The Sword of the LORD with an electronic edge, e-Sword is the go-to place to download a complete Bible study tool onto your computer for free. You can have dozens of Bibles, dictionaries, commentaries, and resource books on your computer available for instant access. This is the program I use and recommend.

Photo Descriptions

The photographs in this book provide a visual of the life and times of Paul and James. These two men lived at the birth of Christianity, when there were no large structures devoted to Christian activity. The big structures they saw (parts of which still survive today) were mostly dedicated to pagan gods and Roman life. What remains helps us imagine what surrounded Paul and James's readers in their everyday lives.

There weren't many, if any, large structures in Galatia during Paul's time and therefore none of the photographs show local life there. Paul, Barnabas, Silas, and Timothy, however, traveled through the cities near Galatia and those photographs do show what they saw. James wrote to all the Jews scattered around the Roman world, and they, too, would see and travel through the areas depicted in the photos.

This annotation list provides brief information about each photograph, and more information is available online.

The Sardis Gymnasium

page 15

The ruins at Sardis are important to the modern traveler, and five photographs from the Sardis area are on pages 15, 23, 49, 51 and 61. The church in Sardis was mentioned in Revelation 1:11; 3:1. This is the front of the large Sardis Gymnasium, which doubled as a school.

Sardis Synagogue

page 23

This is the largest synagogue excavated from during Paul and James's time. Jews worshipping here could have read James's letter. It borders the gymnasium pictured on page 15.

The Temple of Apollo at Delphi

page 17

The oracle at Delphi spoke for the god Apollo and she answered questions from both Greek and foreign visitors. Delphi is not mentioned in the New Testament, but it was operational while Paul was in Greece. The pillars indicate the size of the temple.

Heated Floor

page 35

Large ducts of hot air passed under raised floors in many of the Roman structures to provide heated floors.

The Temple of Apollo at Delphi

page 21

Delphi is not on the coast or a major highway, yet the temple complex had banks and wealth from around the country. This is the setting for the predictions of the oracle of Delphi.

Perga Phamphilia

page 27

This was a beautiful street. Water flowed down the center, and each side was lined by a collanade that provided shade for the storefronts. Paul and Barnabas walked on this street on their way to Antioch of Pisida. (Acts 13:13–14)

Paved Street in Antioch of Pisida

These stones paving the main street in Antioch of Pisida were the stones Paul, Barnabas, Silas, and Timothy passed over as they proclaimed God's word to the Gentiles. (Acts 13)

page 31

Ephesus Library

The Ephesus Library contained more than 1,200 volumes and is indicative of Ephesus's influence in the area. The library was built after Paul ministered in the city.

page 37

Perga of Pamphylia City Gates

Paul and Barnabas passed through these gates on their first missionary journey, and it was breathtakingly beautiful. The gates were four stories tall, and on the inside they were flanked with two walls of life-size marble statues.

page 33

Philippi

The market area in Philippi was surrounded by masonry walls topped by stone columns, which we don't have around our shopping malls today. Philip of Macedon and Alexander the Great passed through Philippi hundreds of years before Paul and Barnabas came.

page 39

Heated Floors

The effort the designers and masons put into heating the floors of some public buildings is impressive.

page 35

When Plans Changed

When plans changed, previous passageways could be blocked off—literally. It appears the stonework over the arch was less than perfect.

page 41

Markets

page 43

The sheer beauty of the marketplaces (details to be filled in by the viewer) included grand colonnades. Pungent fresh produce combined with foreign spices and jewels would have matched any modern shopping center.

Temple of Artemis, Sardis

page 49

This is the fourth largest temple in the ancient world. The columns are five stories tall and the temple was twice the size of the Parthenon in Athens. This temple was 90 miles north of the Great Temple of Artemis in Ephesus (nothing remains of the Ephesus Temple).

Temple of Apollo, Corinth

page 45

In Greek mythology Apollo was the son of Zeus and brother to Artemis (Ephesus and Sardis). He was also associated with the oracle of Delphi. Before Paul's time one thousand prostitutes served in the temple of Aphrodite on top of the mountain in the background.

Sardis Latrine

page 51

Restrooms were required! A stream of water under the seats removed the solids and a smaller stream in front of the seats provided fresh water for the brush, which substituted for toilet paper.

Stone Houses

page 47

In some areas the stone is soft and homes were carved into the hills to provide air conditioning and protection.

Ephesus Grandeur

page 53

Ephesus hosted the seat of government. The regional court was held here, it had a huge theater, it boasted the largest temple to the goddess Artemis, and it was a rich and beautiful city. Paul preached from here for two and a half years.

Column Construction

Without fossil fuel, semi-trucks, or heavy cranes, the construction crews erected thousands of perfectly fitted fluted columns and placed large carved capitals on top of each column. Heavy stone beams connected the columns and the roof was added on top. Amazing!

page 59

Ephesus Theater

With a seating capacity of 25,000, this was the largest theater in the province of Asia. The riot against Paul, which was started by Demetrius the silversmith, was settled in this theater.

page 65

Mosaic Floor, Synagogue of Sardis

The intricate tiled mosaic floors in the Sardis synagogue are evidence of the wealth of the Sardis Jewish community.

page 61

Acropolis of Pergamum

This marketplace must have been gorgeous. It was bordered by a wide street lined with hundreds of stone columns. Within the square the merchandise of the world changed hands.

page 67

Ephesus Columns

One of these two columns has a discolored section. It's easy to speculate whether it was in the original column or selected during restoration. This pair, with their cross member, lines the street leading into Ephesus.

page 63

Columns at Ephesus

These three columns are typical of many restored columns lining the main entry to Ephesus. Many of them mark entrances to Roman Emperor shrines.

page 69

Philippi

From the market square in Philippi one can see the remains of a church that was constructed long after Paul and Silas were arrested here.

page 71

Grandeur in Chunks

Whoever destroyed the beautiful New Testament cities left grandeur in chunks. From these remains we can mentally reconstruct a hint of their former glory.

page 77

Aqueduct Construction

Originally these columns and arches fit together without mortar. The Romans constructed hundreds of miles of roads and aqueducts above arches similar to these.

page 73

About the Author

Dr. Sammons is standing in a doorway which provides a view of Curetes Street in Ephesus. The street is the connection from the upper market to the lower market where Paul worked in Ephesus. The tall building is the Ephesus Library (page 37) which is situated at the junction of Curetes and Marble.

page 80

Temple of Trajan, Pergamum

This is an edge of the Temple of Trajan. It was dedicated to Zeus and Roman Emperor Trajan circa AD 115–130, which was after Paul and James lived.

page 75

Special Thanks

Al Bain

Cindy Baldwin

Gloria Beery

Sean Coons

Max Garrison

William Grant

Richard Halderman

Darnel Hendrickson

Barry Hughes

Peter Lampman

Michel Lauzon

Elizabeth Likes

Luz Lizarraga

Harry Lodge

Doris Loomis

Leigh Anne Lynch

Michael Marcum

Kiely Matthews

Mark Mayers

Wayne & Pam McClafin

Suzanne McQuitty

Helen Wessel Moultrup

Sandy & Chris Neel

Donna & Steve Noxon

Matthew OBrinske

Sally Peel

Earl B. Peterson

Eilene Roecker

Thomas Rose

James Robert Rosenzweig

Anna & Blair Sammons

Garrett Sammons

Kailey Sammons

Phyllis Sammons

Stacy Sammons

Suzy & Steve Sammons

Wesley Sammons

Janet Scarth

Jeff Scott

Olivia Smith

Richard Stahl

R. Todd Swank

Karen Thacker

Sherri Rae Mcclain Westeren

Alexandra Western

Christine Althoff Westhoff

John Wright